Procedures, Techniques, Rules . . .

I Wish I
Learned
in School

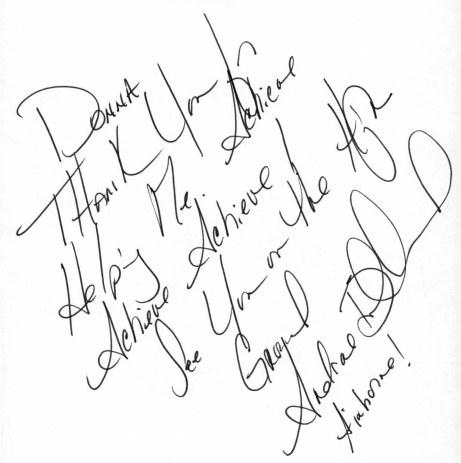

Procedures, Techniques, Rules . . .

I WISH I
LEARNED in
SCHOOL

Andrae Ballard

Alexander Graham Properties LLC, Ohio

Published by Alexander Graham Properties LLC, Ohio

Interior by Dorie McClelland, Spring Book Design
Cover Design by Big Blue Designs

ISBN: 978-0-9906521-0-6
First Edition

This publication contains the author's opinions and is designed to provide accurate information. The author and publisher are not engaged in providing legal, accounting, investment planning, or other professional advice.

To my children, Stori and Chase ~
May your deeds outnumber your desires.

Acknowledgments

I could not have composed this collection without the support and mentoring of many professional and brilliant people who have taken the time to sit with me and impart their knowledge and wisdom. I extend a very special thanks and gratitude to Major Odell Graves, Sarah Ballard, Colonel Benjamin Webb, Lieutenant General John D. Johnson, Colonel Robert P. Ashe, Mitch Shores, L. E. Hewitt, Yancy Greer, Lieutenant Colonel Myles Caggins, Jay Crosby, Fred Fields, Lieutenant Colonel Maria Drew, First Sergeant Zeandrew Farrow, Dr. Joseph Lewis, Colonel William Ostlund, Lieutenant General Daniel Christman, Chief Warrant Officer Desmond Agee, Sergeant Major Joseph Altman, Sergeant First Class Stanley Andrews, Colonel Ross Davidson, Lieutenant Colonel Joseph Scott Peterson, Brigadier General Donald E. Jackson, Brigadier General Neil Tolley, Major Jason Johnson, Major Mark Williams, Major Youngjae Kim, Colonel Stanley Tunstall, Colonel Jacqueline Cumbo, Colonel David Miller, Andre McGlown, Matthew Holzhauer, Lieutenant

Colonel Christopher Budihas, Colonel Brian Mennes, Teresa Ice, Marly Cornell, Ryan Murphy, Adam Macon, David Speed, Felecia Ballard, and Robert Gilmore . . . I am eternally grateful to you each and thank you, for I have gained understanding from your wisdom.

Introduction

I was sitting in my kitchen almost thirteen years ago, having recently been stationed on Oahu, Hawaii, looking through bills, wondering how the amount of my debt got so high in such a short time. After all, just the year before, I graduated from West Point with barely any debt. I was not married nor had I made any major purchases, such as a house, or partnered in a business venture. But I had amassed credit card debt and had absolutely nothing to show for it except some trendy clothes and receipts from every top restaurant in Honolulu. I had always intended to somehow rid myself of the debt, but I found that was more like pushing rope.

My roommates seemed to be in a much better financial situation than I; their sturdy "beater" cars were paid for, while I had a nice convertible with a matching hefty car note. I was furious! No, I was jealous. I asked myself, *What did they know that I didn't?* After all, we all graduated together and had the same jobs in the military. Yet they had financial freedom, while I was definitely a slave to several credit cards and loan repayment schedules.

Early in 2002 my roommate Sean invited his dad to spend a week with us in Hawaii. We made it a point to give Mr. C the full experience of how five bachelor lieutenants lived on the North Shore in paradise. I would say that, between work, barbecues on the beach, and swimming, we gave him plenty of nostalgic reminders of his younger days. I noticed one evening, as he and Sean were sitting on the porch, talking, their dialogue was a peculiar one. Mr. C was doing most of the talking and Sean was scribbling as fast as he could on a notepad. In my mind I wondered, *What kind of father/son talk is this?*

Looking back, I think I was intrigued more than anything else, because I grew up without a father. I had no real clue of what father/son moments really were; I guessed this was one of those moments. I gave them their privacy and made a mental note to ask Sean about it later.

A couple weeks following Mr. C's visit, I asked Sean how his dad thought we were managing with our newly earned independence from college life and acceptance into the workforce. He smiled and said his dad enjoyed himself and was reminded of his youth. I then asked what Sean was writing when he was talking with his dad. He smiled again and said,

"Every bit of wisdom, Drae, is a gem, and I don't want to forget any of it."

At that moment, I realized that my note taking was not yet over, nor was my note taking restricted only to academia. Like my roommate, I needed to take notes on life and capture as many procedures, techniques, and rules from those who have bumped their heads learning and maturing. I had to use those procedures, techniques, and rules as feasible solutions for my life's challenges and make my day-to-day routine as efficient as possible.

I thanked Sean for his advice and for his father's influence. Soon after, I bought a journal and started to capture every procedure, technique, and rule I could find. I decided to chalk up every dollar I had wasted, and now owed, as tuition in the school of life.

Thirteen years later, I had a bundle of notes that I had been using on a day-to-day basis. During that same time, I had three combat deployments in the Middle East, served multiple assignments in the joint special operations community, and was the personal aide to a commanding general. I'm not saying that I did not experience challenges or make mistakes, but I will say that I experienced the added benefits of not making the mistakes I had made preventive notes about. I received rewards from following the guidance of my mentors. Moreover, I found it humbling to see my family members and friends begin to ask me for advice on life, especially guidance on how they could better manage their finances and increase efficiency. What surprised me the most were the challenges I faced in being a parent.

I believe, as a parent, we don't want our children to experience the same painful mistakes we made in our youth; though we understand children must experience life and form their own characters. Like Sean's father, however, if I can provide guiding principles and a solid foundation of honorable values to them, then hopefully, my kids will live life to its fullest potential.

I believe that to whom much is given, much is expected. So I wanted to share these gems of wisdom. I wish I had learned these truths in school, but of course hindsight is 20/20. Some of these procedures, techniques, and rules may seem obvious or like plain common sense. If you already know these truths, then consider yourself fortunate to have already been exposed to them. I encourage you to use these procedures, techniques, and rules, and share them. If you find a few to be enlightening, consider this my gift to you.

I am a proud Christian, and much of my advice has its roots in the Holy Scriptures. I do not mean to offend or to preach, but to let you know my thought process as I wrote my notes and gave them close analysis. Enjoy.

Procedures, Techniques, and Rules

**If an action or decision passes the moral
and ethical standard then . . .
don't think about it.**

Just do it.

Procedure, Technique, and Rule

Stay in prayer.

Procedure, Technique, and Rule

The theory breaks down
when the habit breaks down.

People have good intentions, whether those intentions are to incorporate swimming into their physical fitness regimen or committing to reading for a certain amount of time each day. With good intention, we plan to better ourselves by establishing reoccurring actions that support the accomplishment of our goals. When we fail to accomplish those daily routines that support the overall end state, the idea of the thing we want to accomplish has no support or structure and inevitably fails. So maintain the habit that supports your theory.

Procedure, Technique, and Rule

It's not wrong to be wrong.
It's wrong to stay wrong.

We all make mistakes, but our true character is shown in our ability to correct ourselves and learn from those mistakes. Self-pity should be avoided because no one has time to invest in people who have little-to-no desire to help themselves or who do things that yield low returns.

Procedure, Technique, and Rule

Know that some people can't respect you
past where they first met you . . .
you must push forward in your success.

Recall your mother telling you how fondly she remembers holding you as a child? That is her image of you, her honest and pure child; but the reality is that you are a mature and fully grown adult. Now recall being a teenager who not yet understood how to solve algebra problems, and your peers watched you struggle. You may now teach college-level calculus, but those same peers may still view you as that struggling teen who could not grasp math concepts—they can't move past an impression made years ago, even though you have overcome those challenges and prevailed. Continue in your success anyway.

Procedure, Technique, and Rule

If you don't assign a timeline to goals,
then it's just talk.

I tell my friends and family members often, "Don't talk about it . . . BE about it!" Discussing plans and goals is a good thing; coupling a timeline to those initiatives is the ideal thing.

Procedure, Technique, and Rule

Leaders handle glass balls,
rubber balls, and even plates!

Concerning priorities, leaders not only must judge which balls are glass and which are rubber, leaders now have to become excellent plate spinners. Meaning, our society requires its leaders to oversee multiple "glass" tasks at once.

Procedure, Technique, and Rule

In Philippians 3:13, we are told to forget our past and press ahead.

No one is perfect, and I don't know of a single person who doesn't wish they could go back in time and do something differently—possibly studied more in school, practiced playing an instrument, or nurtured a relationship better. We can't change the past. The only thing we can do is resolve to not make the same mistakes again and ensure that we do better when the next opportunity presents itself.

Procedure, Technique, and Rule

People may not remember your name, but they will remember how you made them feel. Impressions count.

Make good impressions with those you interact with, especially when it comes to first impressions. When those around you see your passion and sincerity, they tend to respect your commitment and if it is logical, are more prone to support your efforts.

Procedure, Technique, and Rule

Ensure that you remain blameless.

Regarding tasks and group efforts, complete your requirement on time. Always go the extra mile in giving support. Do not allow the finger to be pointed at you when the question is asked, "Who was the weakest link in the chain?"

But if you are to blame, accept responsibility, apologize sincerely, and attempt to make amends.

Procedure, Technique, and Rule

Keep your house ten minutes from
being clean at any given time.

Recall those times when you had company over and your home was disorderly and unkempt; you embarrassingly gave your guests a warning or apology in advance. My friend, your preemptive apology is not an excuse, nor does it justify an unacceptable standard. A simple point to wash dishes and clean countertops as you use them. Putting items back in their appropriate places immediately after use will save you time. You can tell a great deal about a person in seeing how they maintain their home. Don't be lazy; clean as you go.

Procedure, Technique, and Rule

Know how to effectively provide analysis.

In giving an analysis you must describe the "what, so what, which means, and therefore." The "therefore" is the most important aspect, because it offers the recommended action to take from the analysis.

Procedure, Technique, and Rule

There is a perfect place to go
when you are broke—to work!

Don't be lazy. Don't sit and wait for the stars to align. Get up, be proactive, humble yourself, and find a job. Some money is better than no money.

Procedure, Technique, and Rule

Do kind things for people,
without telling others about it.

You do not need accolades and praise for everything you do; that in essence is being selfish. Do you really want to give people (to include your family) the impression that you are self-centered?

Procedure, Technique, and Rule

Remember to roll over your
employment 401K plan.

When you leave the job, roll it into your Roth IRA
account. You will have more say so on how to
invest it than if you leave it with a former employer.
Additionally, you increase the amount of investment tracking over the long term if you leave it
with an employer; ten jobs yield ten potential 401K
resources that you have to keep track of annually.
Avoid the hassle by rolling them into your personal
IRA when you leave the job.

Procedure, Technique, and Rule

Know the difference between
circle of influence and circle of concern.

Within a circle of influence are things you directly
can affect at the time, such as the agenda of a meeting. Whereas within a circle of concern are things
you cannot directly affect, such as realizing you left
the lights on at home while you were already con-
ducting your meeting.

Procedure, Technique, and Rule

Commit yourself to being the hardest and
smartest working person in the room.
What would you do differently at work
if God were your boss?

Yes, you become the "go to" person. But that is a
good thing. In developing a reputation hinged on
dependability you will learn how to be exact and
precise as you answer the mail. It will take time
to perfect your actioned efficiency but you will do
it. General officers are professionals at this. They
are able to handle many strategic problem-sets at
rapid pace because they rely on their experiences.
As you detangle issues in your workplace know
that you are honing your problem-solving skills
(as they associate with time as well).

Procedure, Technique, and Rule

Form should follow function.

Just don't do things for the sake of doing things.
Have a purpose.

Procedure, Technique, and Rule

If you rest, you rust. No matter how you
feel, get up, dress up, and show up.

I often wondered, *How is it that school teachers
teach for forty years and then at retirement, tutor and
remain in the education environment?* I realize now
that staying active allows for their minds and body
to be challenged and engaged in effort to preserve
their sharp intellect and fitness.

Procedure, Technique, and Rule

It is okay to outgrow your friends.

Everybody who came with you may not be able to go with you! Sometimes the people who grew up with you will not be ready to move with you toward your endeavors. They may even hinder your journey to success. Keep your eyes on the prize, and push toward your goals.

Procedure, Technique, and Rule

The squeaky wheel gets the grease.

Voice your challenges to the environment's decision makers. But when you do so, be sure to also provide feasible solutions. Many people can cite discrepancies and issues, but true influential people offer possible solutions to those challenges.

Procedure, Technique, and Rule

The plan is not nearly as important as the planning.

In the Army, we say that most plans don't survive first contact, meaning our plans are hardly ever executed exactly how we estimated; they morph. With careful planning however, all parties should have a clear idea of what the final product should look like. Because you have already identified the critical functions from the noncritical functions, as a result of the planning process, you know where to focus efforts as factors change your plan. So plan your work, and then work your plan.

Procedure, Technique, and Rule

If you are gonna be a bear,
then be a grizzly.

If you are going to be that force to reckon with, do not be shy or gullible. Be bold with your efforts.

Procedure, Technique, and Rule

You don't have to always be in charge.

Sometimes you have to shut up and color. Every good leader was once a follower. It's always a good practice to observe and learn from others.

Procedure, Technique, and Rule

True wealth is having time
and the freedom to maneuver.

Whereas money is the tangible asset that describes your economic energy, the less energy you have means the less freedom and ability you have to maneuver. Utilize your assets wisely, because you cannot get back time, and people have died for your freedom. Make your money work for you. Using it correctly over time will reward you with more freedom to maneuver.

Procedure, Technique, and Rule

Get it out of your mind that this
world owes you something.
Don't expect something for nothing.
Life isn't fair, but it's still good.

As parents, we want our children to grow up and
be mature, productive, independent adults. Whatever our situation is, we can improve it. Have the
mind-set that you will not wait for someone to
help you. Start by helping yourself. Doing so will
show your discipline and in turn, people who can
assist your efforts can do so without feel like they
are being misused.

Procedure, Technique, and Rule

Do not pass a penny, nickel, dime,
or quarter lying in the street.

Bench your pride. Pick it up and put it in the bank.
You're that much closer to your financial goal.

Procedure, Technique, and Rule

Do NOT smoke.

We know that health studies show the risks you assume when you smoke. Think on how you offend others with the smell. The smell stays on your clothes, even though you've gone outside to the designated smoking area . . . and yes, though they may not say anything aloud, people are hoping to get away from the smell as soon as possible.

Procedure, Technique, and Rule

Plan to have grocery money
left over at the end of the week.

Since the cost of groceries tends to fluctuate at any
given time, plan a week in advance for what you
are going to cook and eat. Buy your groceries no
more than once a week. Cook enough food to last
your household at least two days. That way, you can
cook less often. Chicken, potatoes, and spaghetti
go a long way. Do not bring your credit or debit
card to the grocery store; do not even have it in the
car while you run inside—you might find yourself
running outside to get it. Bottom line: Leave your
credit and debit cards at home, and only take cash,
a calculator, coupons, and your shopping list into
the store. Plan your budget to spend less than you
have. If your allocation is $100 a week for grocer-
ies, plan to spend only $85.

Procedure, Technique, and Rule

Realize that another person's anger
may not be about you.

For example, in some situations, your boss will be mad at "the chair"—not at you. Some positions come with responsibilities that are extremely serious and emotional. Military officers for example, face adjudicating punishments for theft, abuse, and misuse, and it can be overwhelming when mishaps come frequently. Your supervisor may appear curt or busy, not because he or she dislikes you, but because handling a multitude of things that their job (the chair) requires can create pressure.

Procedure, Technique, and Rule

Do not lease a car . . .
and do not lease a car to own.

I received this advice from a car salesman. Do not
buy a brand new car . . . instead buy in cash, a two-
or three-year-old car. He emphasized that car sales-
people aim to get the lowest trade-in price for your
vehicle. He suggested that when you trade in a car at
a dealership, look at a very expensive car first, and
offer your trade-in for that expensive car. The car
dealer's main focus is to get you in a new car at pre-
mium cost, so he will be more inclined to give you
optimum value on your trade-in. So do not look at
a used car first; if you are trading in a car, get the
trade-in value first.

Procedure, Technique, and Rule

Appoint an attorney as the
executor of your estate
if there is going to be
more than one beneficiary.

List your assets and store them in a place that anyone can locate when the time comes. Ensure that the envelope is sealed. I recommend having four or five identical copies, all dated and notarized at the same time with instructions included that indicate that there are multiple identical copies, and this is copy #X out of however many copies were made. Doing so ensures that, in the event of your passing, your will can be retrieved quickly and with no restructuring of its intent, because multiple parties are aware.

Procedure, Technique, and Rule

Never tell your kids that you are wealthy.

I believe this to be one of the most important things that may help you in raising children. Without the knowledge of your wealth, they will not feel as though they are entitled to anything. Let them work hard for and earn everything they have. For example, if you knew that your college tuition was paid for to the college of your choice, would you work extra hard to ensure that your grades were good enough to get in? For the majority, the answer to this question is "Probably not." The student that has no sense of entitlement will study harder to ensure that their grades are solid in order to secure a good scholarship.

Procedure, Technique, and Rule

Utilize the steam room/sauna
as often as you can.

A good sweat in the sauna or steam room is the best form in cleaning out your pores and is typically a good place to think in quiet peace. When I was a boy, my uncle would sit in the steam room for fifteen to twenty minutes, shaving, while I could only stay in there for a couple of minutes. Over time, I built up the ability to endure the heat. Now, I make it a point to steam daily and shave in the steam room at every opportunity . . . my pores remain clean, my complexion is clear, and I leave the steam room with a more concise plan of action.

Procedure, Technique, and Rule

Gold and silver are a storehouse of wealth.

They are better than fiat currency, because they are tangible and they protect purchasing power. Keep them in your safe, safety deposit box, or under your mattress, and you will find security in holding your hard-earned wealth. Thrift stores are excellent venues to find sterling silver (eating utensils and jewelry) that you can cash in for melt value.

Procedure, Technique, and Rule

Save every five dollar bill in a separate
savings account.

I find it interesting to discover different ways to challenge myself in saving money. When I receive a five dollar bill as change from a transaction I ensure that I deposit it in my savings account. You will be surprised how fast that grows. The kicker is when the cashier gives you multiple five dollar bills as change; that's bittersweet at times.

Procedure, Technique, and Rule

The grass is not greener
over here or over there.
It's greener where YOU water it.

If you invest the necessary time and energy into your own endeavors, they will be just as fruitful. Plus, you never know what the others are sacrificing in order to maintain outward appearances. They may have the big house, fancy car, and nice clothes, but at the same time be filing bankruptcy or struggling to keep the lights on.

Procedure, Technique, and Rule

Postdate money orders and checks
for later use.

For a specific item or time, such as anniversaries or birthdays, save money throughout the year via money orders that are made out to you and postdated to the date that you need them. Money orders are typically good for a year, cost a few cents at your local grocery store, and don't lose their face value. Postdate the money order so that you can't take it to the bank prematurely and use the funds for something unplanned.

Procedure, Technique, and Rule

Information fuels the
decision-making process.

Yes, General Patton said that he'd rather execute
a good plan violently than execute a perfect plan
next week. Timing was more critical to him than
a fully thought-out scheme of maneuver. In your
workplace there might be instances where you will
not have the entire scope of effect captured, yet
you must make a decision for the betterment of
your organization. This is why the leaders have the
associated titles. You must take the given information you have and execute your task; being sure to
mitigate risk along the way. With the information
you do have, be sure that it is accurate, timely, precise, usable, and reliable.

Procedure, Technique, and Rule

Always keep potatoes in the pantry.

You can cook many variations, from potato wedges to mashed potatoes, or add them to dishes, such as eggs and salads.

Procedure, Technique, and Rule

Stop whining and do something productive.

It has always been my belief that the time and energy you waste crying over a situation could easily be used for more productive activities, such as figuring out a solution to your problem.

Procedure, Technique, and Rule

Tie a knot at the end of your shoelaces,
so they will not come out of the shoe hole.

You will appreciate this bit of advice more when
you have kids. I can't tell you how many hours I've
wasted trying to lace shoes with shredded shoelaces. Tying the knot keeps the lace in the shoe and
it also maintains the integrity of the lace.

Procedure, Technique, and Rule

True inflation is
the increase of currency supply,
and rising costs are merely
the governing body's reaction.

For example, if we say that a loaf of bread costs $1.00 yet we increase money supply, though the physical value of the bread is $1.00, the actual cost of the bread will be inflated to meet the proportion of the increase in money supply. Recall the cost of a loaf of bread forty years ago and compare it to the cost of bread now.

Procedure, Technique, and Rule

Know the difference between your assets, liabilities, and expenses.

Assets generate positive cash flow into your wallet and have no lien held against them; they are owned free and clear. Liabilities have a significant risk attached to the product, though they might carry equity; mortgages fall into this category. If your property is valued at $300K and you owe $175K, your home is still a liability because you have a lien against the title with the mortgage lender. Money is leaving your pocket, because monthly you are paying the mortgage lender principle and interest on the loan. Your property becomes an asset when you have paid the debt off in full. Expenses are reoccurring; if you own a phone, you will have a monthly phone bill. Operate to accumulate assets, eliminate liabilities, and reduce operating expenses.

Procedure, Technique, and Rule

Know that implementing good discipline is
the bridge between setting your goals
and accomplishing them.

Start by capturing the task/goal over the speci-
fied period of time and couple it with the person
assigned to accomplish the responsibility. The *discipline* aspect is the key component to achieving
the goal. I encourage you to break down your goals
into sub-goals that support your overall initiative;
this will keep you on a glide path for success.

Procedure, Technique, and Rule

Concerning anger, be sure never
to wrestle with pigs because,
when you do, know that
everyone gets dirty—
and pigs like being dirty anyways.

Recall your times dealing with difficult people and
how emotionally and mentally drained you felt
when you parted. Did you make any gains from
the argument? Realize that arguing with people
who enjoy chaos and disorder yields no positive
outcome because your purpose is to improve a
situation while theirs is to instigate emotional
tension.

Procedure, Technique, and Rule

Do not remove tags from clothing
and other purchased items
until you use them.

You never know if you will need to return, exchange, or resell the item. Keep the associated receipts. If you have misplaced the receipt, stores are more inclined to honor your return with store credit or a full refund upon scanning the price tag barcode.

Procedure, Technique, and Rule

Perform under adversity.

Know that diamonds are made with pressure. Your mind-set should be "Let's stop talking and advance the ball . . . do something!"

Procedure, Technique, and Rule

Operate with integrity
despite outside influences.
Dwell in the band of excellence.

Everyone you encounter will not have the same
moral and ethical values you have. Maintain your
high output standards and always do what is right
. . . even when no one is looking.

Procedure, Technique, and Rule

Life isn't tied with a bow, but it's still a gift.
Believe in miracles. Get outside every day.
Miracles are waiting everywhere.

Your situation could always be worse so be thankful for the things you do have. Everyone enjoys comfort and security, and your environment does not dictate what you can be. Remember that it is not always about the culmination. The journey is your testimony.

Procedure, Technique, and Rule

If you see someone without a smile,
give him/her one.

Your smile or kind gesture may be the only pleas-
ant thing he or she has received after a series of
unfortunate events. It will give comfort in seeing
that not everyone is an antagonist.

Procedure, Technique, and Rule

The only stupid question is
the question that is not asked.

Your question or explanation may generate a light-
bulb moment for someone in the audience.

Procedure, Technique, and Rule

Do not use a lot of salt.

Excessive sodium contributes to high blood pressure, which causes the heart to work harder to circulate blood throughout the body. Realizing and implementing this at an older age is too late. The added workload on the heart coupled with the added pressure on the heart can lead to heart failure or stroke. Excessive sodium can also lead to cirrhosis or liver disease.

Procedure, Technique, and Rule

If you are not sure of what you
want to do after you graduate from high
school, consider military service.

If accepted, you can join and use that time to
gather yourself while serving your country. You
will also gain leadership experience, improve your
skill set, develop your physical condition, and
form long-lasting relationships with people from
all over the world.

Procedure, Technique, and Rule

Try to drink a gallon of water a day.

Secondary effects, other than keeping you hydrated, include flushing impurities from your body, increased energy, healthier skin, and fat loss. If you fall just short of a gallon, it is okay because you are building a habit of good health awareness.

Procedure, Technique, and Rule

Always consider recommendations.

Experience is a cruel teacher. It gives you the test first, and then the lesson; but you do get a cheat sheet . . . it's heeding the mentorship and guidance of the wise.

Procedure, Technique, and Rule

Forgive.

Bad experiences with churches or people might deserve another try. After all, you've probably had a bad experience with a car, and I bet you still drive one.

Procedure, Technique, and Rule

Use cash . . . you can bargain.

Do not take the cashier's word that they can't grant unadvertised discounts without first speaking to a decision maker . . . a manager. I have explored discounts, price-matching alternatives (I prefer asking the manager to beat the competitor's price in order to gain my business). No, you are not being a cheapskate; you are however, being thrifty; and every penny not spent, but saved, is added to your accumulation of wealth.

Procedure, Technique, and Rule

To get something you never had,
you gotta do something you've never done.

We have all heard, "To repeatedly do something
and hope for a different outcome is the action of
an insane individual." So change your actions to
obtain a different outcome. Yes, it may be uncom-
fortable and require more energy, but if you achieve
your goal as a result, count it all joy and accept that
it was needed to be done.

Procedure, Technique, and Rule

Have everyone on board with the vision.

When everyone on the team is fully engaged, better decisions are made. At the same time, when everyone on the team is committed, it is hard to let dumb courses of action pass. If a team member expresses apprehension or disagreement about a particular plan, ask for feasible alternatives.

Procedure, Technique, and Rule

Keep toothpaste, floss, and a toothbrush
in the shower with you.

You might as well brush while you're in there. I
know this may sound crazy, but you would be surprised how many people do not brush their teeth
more than once a day, so give yourself the added
opportunity.

Procedure, Technique, and Rule

Keep a "Get Home Bag" in your car.

If your car ever brakes down, having a flashlight, a few dollars, an emergency blanket, flares, bottled water, and a disposable camera, among other things, readily available will prove beneficial.

Procedure, Technique, and Rule

Max out your ROTH IRA as soon as you
start earning taxable income . . .
and do NOT touch it until the
minimum retirement age.

The level of comfort you will have in your retirement depends on the moves you make and habits
you form early in life. If you are not implementing a plan for success in retirement you surely will
have an outcome of failure.

Procedure, Technique, and Rule

The best time to purchase Christmas gift wrapping paper is the day after Christmas.

Plan early, buy it at the extreme discount and use it for next year's holiday season. With anything, stores charge premiums on in-season items.

Procedure, Technique, and Rule

Spend the interest . . . never the principle.

Just do it.

Procedure, Technique, and Rule

Freedom in a relationship is
a direct reflection of order.

Mutual understanding of loyalty and respect in a relationship enables you to have the freedom to socialize in good taste and without question or concern.

Procedure, Technique, and Rule

Bend the will without breaking the spirit . . .
understand partnering.

Encourage team members to share information and offer your team members opportunities to lead. Remember that the most effective team leaders build their relationships based on trust and loyalty, rather than fear or the power of their positions.

Procedure, Technique, and Rule

It is good courtesy to send a handwritten thank-you note when you receive a gift.

Sending a handwritten note is becoming more of a lost art nowadays, but it is still a major indicator of one's appreciation. Technology enables you to automate responses at the click of a mouse button, therefore callusing your gratitude, but taking the time to personalize a message shows your sincerity and gratitude.

Procedure, Technique, and Rule

Being overweight is not acceptable.

Sometimes you need to hear the truth without soft mittens. No matter what physical condition you are in, work toward getting yourself in better shape. Being in the best physical condition helps you; for example, healthier people tend to recover quicker from injuries. I am not attempting to belittle those who are overweight. I am, however, reinforcing and actively promoting the importance of a healthy lifestyle, and I am encouraging you to do something productive about your physical condition.

Procedure, Technique, and Rule

Life is short—enjoy it.

Ask yourself at the end of each day if you did every-thing you could with the time you had. If the answer is no, then I guess you have a few more things to do before bedding down. Do not be lazy and do not put off tomorrow what you can do today.

Procedure, Technique, and Rule

Your job won't take care of you when you
are sick. Your friends and family will.

I'm not saying leave your job when you get sick. I
am encouraging you to remember to nurture your
relationships and help people.

Procedure, Technique, and Rule

Build an emergency savings . . . then grow it to the amount equivalent to six months or a year of necessary expenses.

Put the money in a plastic sandwich bag and then place the bag inside a soup can. Fill the soup can with water and keep it in your freezer. Only take it out in a true emergency. With this method, you have to take the time to thaw it out. (You can't stick a soup can in a microwave.) This method will force you to think twice before spending your emergency money.

Procedure, Technique, and Rule

You don't have to win every argument.
Stay true to yourself.

You may be correct in your opinion, but have you stopped to consider that there might be another viable solution? Take refuge in being confident in your logic. To win or push your opinion in every conversation could also show that you are not open for creativity and suggestions. The affect is that you turn off those around you and even worse, you foster a work environment that does not cultivate creativity which may reduce efficiency.

Procedure, Technique, and Rule

Make peace with your past so it won't
screw up the present and future.

When your mother told you not to burn bridges, she knew what she was talking about. Think on those times, when you ended a relationship on bad terms and then needed a resource that person had. At that point you saw how you could (and should) have handled the relationship. Moreover, you don't know how people might help you along your way. For example, the person you offend one day just might be in a room with your supervisor, someone you may be interested in, or on a board of directors that decides an action that directly affects you. Consider how easy it is for that person to drop seeds of discontent about you. Bottom line: Treat people the way you want to be treated.

Procedure, Technique, and Rule

It's okay to let your children see you cry,
just not too often.

Emotions are a normal part of life. Both tears of joy
and tears of grief all will happen from time to time.
It is important that our children understand that it
is okay to show our emotions but in excess may be
a catalyst for anxiety and worry.

Procedure, Technique, and Rule

Don't compare your life to others.

You have no idea what their journey is. Envy is a waste of time. Be appreciative of what you already have, not dwell on what you want. Remember for very level of success, there is a devil trying to debunk you. So stay in your lane and put your attention on achieving your goal. Once you achieve it, set another and let that occupy your time.

Procedure, Technique, and Rule

If a relationship has to be a secret,
you shouldn't be in it.

No negotiations.

Procedure, Technique, and Rule

Everything can change in the
blink of an eye,
but don't worry, God never blinks.

You have no idea what the future holds for you.
Surely you can speculate with very high probability in different instances, but their are factors that
you cannot have 100 percent certainty. Football
players who are at the peak of their career cannot
predict a tackle that will cause them injury enough
to prematurely end a promising career; yet it happens often. In the same scenario, other doors can
and will open for you which because of your previous endeavors have postured you for even greater
success.

Procedure, Technique, and Rule

Just be there.

Sometimes the best you should do for someone is be present. From graduations, games and recitals to funerals, briefings, and rehearsals. You are not expected to provide anything other than your attention, showing selfless support for someone else's cause.

Procedure, Technique, and Rule

Get rid of anything that isn't useful.
Clutter weighs you down in many ways.

If you have not used it in six months to a year, it probably can go in the *Donate to Charity* pile. Also avoid toxic people because they rob you of your potential, energy, and time.

Procedure, Technique, and Rule

Whatever doesn't kill you
really does make you stronger.

Use your trials and tribulations as testimony to how perseverance and intestinal fortitude gave you what you needed to make it through adversity.

Procedure, Technique, and Rule

Do not allow yourself to be complacent.

Each day is a new opportunity to excel.
The best is yet to come.

Procedure, Technique, and Rule

Fight for your equities.

When it comes to going after what you love in life,
don't take no for an answer.

Procedure, Technique, and Rule

Over prepare, and then go with the flow.

Recall the confidence and comfort you had when you were prepared for something. In contrast, remember how apprehensive or timid you felt when you were not postured for success. It is always better to be ready and go with the flow, than to not be ready and still be forced to go forward.

Procedure, Technique, and Rule

Always keep flip flops in your gym bag.

Purchase an inexpensive pair at your local convenience store. They pay you dividends each time you shower in a public facility as well as when you leave the gym and don't want to put on socks and sneakers.

Procedure, Technique, and Rule

Frame every so-called disaster
with this question:
In five years, will this matter?

Think back five years ago and recall those so-called crisis moments. Some may be legitimate, but I'm sure there are those that do not qualify as disasters. Though at the time, we (through our emotions) saw and categorized them as pretty stressful. I encourage you to be proactive in asking if this so-called disaster will truly matter in the coming years. Still handle the challenge, but do so in efforts to prevent a crisis escalation.

Procedure, Technique, and Rule

Do something to put a smile on God's face.

Live so that you become associated with terms as selfless, integrity, kind, wise, and humble. Remember you are what you do, not what you say.

Procedure, Technique, and Rule

Give time time.

Time heals almost everything.

Procedure, Technique, and Rule

However good or bad a situation is,
it will change.

One thing in this world is for certain—that things change. We grow from young to old, have good days and bad days, win games, and unfortunately lose games. No matter what your situation is bear through it and know that you will have a wonderful testimony of your perseverance. Use the memories of your triumphs to give assurance that you will have a better day.

Procedure, Technique, and Rule

Don't take yourself so seriously.
No one else does.

If our society jokes about its presidents, governors, priests, and other professionals, do you really think that you are exempt? There is a difference in tasks at hand however. There are times when you must be extremely serious and focused. For example, a doctor performing surgery must be committed to focused excellence; at the same time, he should otherwise be able to laugh at his own personal imperfections, which others might find humorous as well.

Procedure, Technique, and Rule

God loves you because of who God is,
not because of anything you did or didn't do.

Accept it.

Procedure, Technique, and Rule

Know how to give an elevator summary
when describing a little about yourself.

Be concise and efficient in your dialogue and
explanations. Try to make your delivery in about
the time of an elevator ride or a walk to your mail-
box and back. This will force you to be extremely
exact in your comments. It is not a "canned"
delivery; it should however be very familiar.

Procedure, Technique, and Rule

Growing old beats the alternative
of dying young.

Cherish our more senior relatives for the wisdom and experiences they have to share. So many people die at younger ages due to sickness, accidents, or tragic events; they miss out on life's opportunities. Enjoy growing old because you get to take part in an exciting journey.

Procedure, Technique, and Rule

It is not practice makes perfect.
It is perfect practice makes perfect.

We are not perfect; we can never be. There is one thing we can do: Practice. Constant endeavors to pursue excellence is the mind-set we should have. Though we are not perfect, we can dwell in the band of excellence by holding ourselves, coworkers, family members, and friends accountable to a high standard. Think about those times when field goal kickers practice for that one critical kick during football games. Their practice day is nothing more than rehearsed routine. The kicker practices one motion 40 to 100 times a day. He critiques his foot placement, body position, and required momentum of his kick. He does this every day all week so that come game day his kicks are felt just like practice.

Procedure, Technique, and Rule

Know how to fish.

Fishing is a life skill. It offers an excellent opportunity to spend quality time with family, bonding and creating life-long memories. It enhances the appreciation of the natural world while providing a teaching opportunity of water and boating safety rules.

Procedure, Technique, and Rule

If you are going to go to the gym,
get a sweat.

If you leave the gym without fatiguing your muscles, you wasted your time and money going. Check your ego at the gym door, improve your health, improve and strengthen your heart. Have fun and socialize there, but do not lose focus of its intended purpose. Recall those people at the gym, who stay there three hours talking and joking while doing only a few push-ups with a thirty-second stretch as an afterthought. They have the nerve to boast to their friends as if their fitness regimen was a result of their practices and (questionable) good health. Their efforts are lukewarm and, when exposed, leave their words moot. The main purpose for a fitness center is to provide you with a means to improve your physical fitness; so seize its opportunity.

Procedure, Technique, and Rule

Keep a journal of your memoirs.

Tell your story and give your words of wisdom. Describe your challenges and explain how you overcame them. At the very least, you have captured your thoughts for others (your descendants especially) to read and appreciate.

Procedure, Technique, and Rule

Close the loop.

Verify everything. For example, knowing when your property taxes are due, use your calendar reminder to call your mortgage lender two weeks prior to ensure they are aware of the pending payment due, and then call the county tax authority a week after to ensure they received the payment. Never put your destiny in someone else's hands. Contact all participating parties to ensure your desired end state has been met. I call it closing the loop.

Procedure, Technique, and Rule

Do routine things routinely
by putting your routine on automatic.

Use your electronic calendar to set reminders for birthday emails or cards, date nights, bill payments, credit report checks, and property tax payments, to name a few. Be sure to schedule them on a reoccurring timeline. Automatic investments can be made via your banking institution. Automatic bill payment should be scheduled to come out the day your wages deposit into your checking account. Check your credit history with the credit bureaus every year during your birth month. Schedule it on your calendar now, and set it to reoccur annually.

Procedure, Technique, and Rule

Begin discussions and contemplation with the question, "If you had it your way, how would you spend twenty-four hours?"

Then ask, "What is preventing you from achieving that ideal day?"

Then ask, "What are you doing to fix it?" Do this, to gain perspective of your time and its value. Never waste a second that could be used for self-development. When this is realized, you will find that you will have little tolerance for those things that waste your time and energy; and there is nothing wrong with that.

Procedure, Technique, and Rule

Avoid credit card use.

Instead, save and pay with cash. Before credit cards were in existence Americans saved up to make purchases or did without (I bet people's debt-to-income ratio back then was a great deal lower as well—I'm just saying). If you ask your intelligent aunt or your wise grandfather, they will tell you to avoid credit cards like the plague. Credit cards are the quickest way to get yourself in a spending frenzy, thereby increasing your debt.

Procedure, Technique, and Rule

If you must have a credit card,
pay it off every month.

Doing so demonstrates that
you understand priorities.

Doing so, means you do not increase
your debt balance.

Doing so builds your credit score.

Get the point?

Procedure, Technique, and Rule

At a social function,
consider ordering soup and/or salad.

The cost is usually lower and the food is generally
healthier, while just as filling.

Procedure, Technique, and Rule

Your mortgage should never be any more than three times your annual household gross (minus 15 percent) salary.

Save until your down payment allows this to happen. Do not fall into the trap of competing with your colleagues who appear to have riches and glamour. A large $450K home with 4,000 square feet and two extra-large water heaters has all the bells and whistles, but it also has a reoccurring electricity bill to heat and cool all that space and other maintenance requirements that come along with that mansion. Keep your mortgage under control with a larger down payment or a smaller house.

Procedure, Technique, and Rule

All that truly matters in the end
is that you loved.

When we die and cross the *Great Divide*, we cannot take any money, gold, pictures, or clothes. What will be your legacy? You are a memory to those whom you influenced. How do you want to be remembered?

Procedure, Technique, and Rule

Open up conversations with,
"What is the best piece of advice
you have ever received?"

and then offer yours.

My Wish to You

I wish you success. Moreover, I wish for you to accept nothing less than success. To all who have learned the hard way, hopefully these techniques will help you in your day-to-day routines. Some people are fortunate enough to have a wise role model who they can go to for the answers to life's trials. But there are those who may not have anyone they can rely on for mentorship. Wherever you fall in the spectrum, I hope this book will confirm your habits or set a spark for other positive habits to be initiated. Our habits define who we are. No matter what, set yourself up for success—and help someone else with theirs.

I'll see you on the high ground.

About the Author

Andrae Ballard is a graduate of the United States Military Academy at West Point where he was commissioned as an Infantry Officer. With nearly fifteen years of military service, he has served at every echelon from platoon through Corps level operations. He is also a part-time faculty member at Central Texas College, teaching in the Mathematics Department. He holds a BS in Systems Engineering from West Point and an MS from Central Michigan University in Human Resources Administration.

Andrae's most recent assignments include serving as the Aide-de-Camp to the 8th Army Commanding General in Yongsan, Korea, as well as the Public Affairs Officer for the Special Operations Command Korea Commanding General and the 1st Armored Brigade Combat Team, 3rd Infantry Division in Fort Stewart, Georgia. He has been a Brigade Communications Officer for the 1st Heavy Brigade Combat Team, 2nd Infantry Division in Camp Hovey, Korea, as well as for the 1st Battalion, 75th Ranger Regiment at Hunter Army Airfield, Georgia. His deployments include multiple combat tours in Operation Iraqi Freedom and Operation Enduring Freedom (Afghanistan).

Andrae is a graduate of the United States Army Command and General Staff College, as well as the United States Army Jumpmaster and Ranger Schools. He is the president of Alexander Graham Properties LLC, an organization that provides resources and consultation to those in need of financial help.

Andrae has spoken throughout the world, helping people to hone their leadership skills and potential and has assisted many, helping them to establish a clear and effective strategy to meet their life goals.

Andrae Ballard
PO Box 739
Ashburn, Virginia 20146
Achieve@AndraeBallard.com
www.AndraeBallard.com

CPSIA information can be obtained at www.ICGtesting.com
Printed in the USA
LVOW07s1334270515

440097LV00001B/6/P